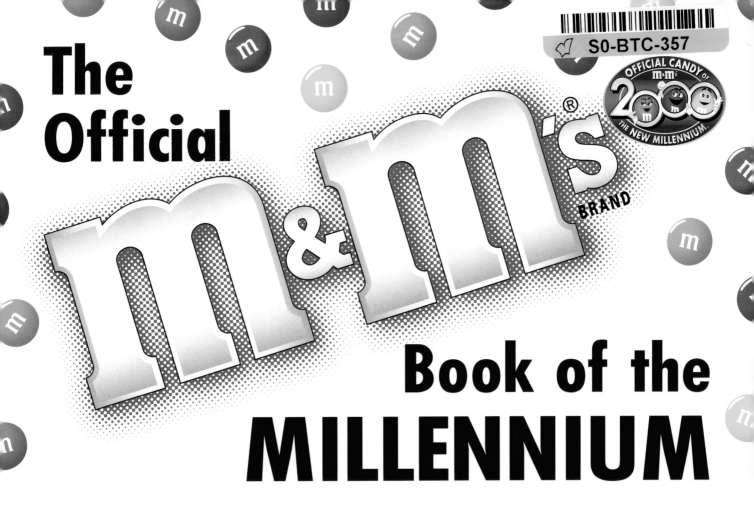

The Official m&m's BRAND

Book of the MILLENNIUM

Larry Dane Brimner • illustrated by Karen E. Pellaton

This is an important date!

31 DECEMBER 1999

1 JANUARY 2000

Charlesbridge

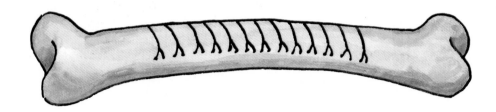

To Sheila Cole, Jean Ferris, and Kathy Krull—writers for a new millennium
–L. D. B.

To my favorite filmmaker, Gretchen
–K. E. P.

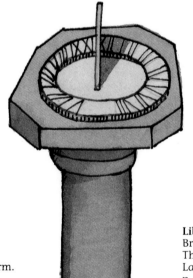

Text © 1999 by Larry Dane Brimner
Illustrations © 1999 by Karen E. Pellaton
All rights reserved, including the right of
reproduction in whole or in part in any form.

Published by Charlesbridge Publishing
85 Main Street
Watertown, MA 02472
(617) 926-0329
www.charlesbridge.com

Printed in South Korea
(hc) 10 9 8 7 6 5 4 3 2 1
(sc) 10 9 8 7 6 5 4 3 2 1

™/® M&M's, M and the M&M's Characters are
trademarks of Mars, Incorporated or its affiliates.
© Mars, Inc. 1999.
Manufactured and distributed under
license by Charlesbridge Publishing.

Library of Congress Cataloging-in-Publication Data
Brimner, Larry Dane.
The official "M&M's"® book of the millennium /
Larry Dane Brimner; illustrated by Karen E. Pellaton.
p.   cm.
ISBN 0-88106-071-2 (reinforced for library use)
ISBN 0-88106-072-0 (softcover)
1. Time—Juvenile literature. 2. Calendar—Juvenile
literature. I. Pellaton, Karen E. II. Title. III. Title:
Official "M&M's"® book of the millennium.
QB209.5.B75   1999
529'.2—dc21   99-19359
                                                          CIP

The illustrations in this book were done in
watercolor on Arches watercolor paper "hot press".
The display type and text type were set in Futura,
Publicity Gothic, and Stone Informal.
Color separations were made by Sung In Printing,
Inc., South Korea.
Printed and bound by Sung In Printing, Inc.,
South Korea
Production supervision by Brian G. Walker
Designed by Diane M. Earley

Everyone is Excited about the New Millennium!
Get Ready to Celebrate!

Great!
I love parties!

Uh, what
is a
millennium?

A millennium is an amount of time, a **big** amount
of time. Before people, there were no days, weeks,
months, or years. Then people came along and needed
to measure time. We've been doing it ever since.

Some small amounts of time were easy to decide on
and understand. A day was the time from one sunrise
or sunset to the next. The time between market days
became what we now call a week. Months changed
with the return of the new moon. A year? Usually this
was the time from one spring to the next, from one fall
to the next, or in Egypt, from one flood to the next.

TIME, WORDS,

People have often needed to keep track of larger amounts of time, too, and invented words for them. Today, we call 10 years a decade. A person who is 10 years old is also 1 decade old. A century is 10 decades, or 100 years.

And we say 1,000 years is one millennium.

I'm all out of fingers.

These words have roots in other languages. *Decade* came from the Greek *deka*, meaning "ten." *Century* and *millennium* came from the Romans, who spoke Latin: *centuria*, meaning "a group of one hundred," and *mill*, meaning "one thousand."

We also borrowed something else from the Romans: Roman numerals. Sometimes they are still carved into cornerstones of public buildings to mark the year they were built.

What Roman numeral might you find in the cornerstone of a building built in the year 2000? **MM**—the mark of the new millennium, a move from the 1000s to the 2000s.

MM—Look, that's us!

ACME BUILDING MCMX

AND NUMBERS

MM is a tidy way to write the year 2000, but Roman numerals are not always tidy.

MM=2000

It's GREEK to me.

Actually it's ROMAN.

The longest year so far, in the number of Roman numerals, was 1888: MDCCCLXXXVIII. Thirteen numerals long!

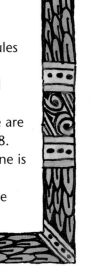

ROMAN NUMERALS

Roman numerals are letters of the alphabet that stand for numbers:

I (1), V (5), X (10), L (50),
C (100), D (500), M (1000).

The letters are strung together to add up to a number. Like this:

II = 2 (1 + 1)   VII = 7 (5 + 1 + 1)
        XXX = 30 (10 + 10 + 10)
IX = 9 (10 - 1)   MM = 2000 (1000 + 1000)

Why isn't the number 9 written as VIIII (5 + 1 + 1 + 1 + 1)?
No one knows for sure, but there are rules that apply to all Roman numerals:
- Always start with the biggest numeral possible.
- Numerals to the right of a bigger one are added. So VIII (5 + 1 + 1 + 1) equals 8.
- The numeral on the left of a bigger one is subtracted. So IX (10 - 1) equals 9.
- A numeral may be repeated only three times in a row.

Now I Know What a Millennium Is!
. . . Why Is the Millennium Now?

That's a long—but interesting—story. Can you remember everything you did yesterday or last week, or are some of those things forgotten history? Imagine what it would be like trying to keep track of an event that happened 50, 100, or 1000 years ago. People need to remember events of the past and to plan for the future, and so they count the years.

CHINESE CALENDAR FOR THE YEAR 4698

To keep track, people invented *calendars*. But calendars start at different times. The Chinese calendar is one of the longest-running calendars in history, beginning in the 2600s B.C., when Emperor Huang Ti introduced it. By this calendar, the year 2000 will be 4698.

What's B.C.?

Before candy?

The Islamic calendar began in A.D. 622—a way of remembering Mohammed's journey from Mecca to Medina. As a result, in the year of the new millennium, the Muslim calendar will reach the year 1420.

The Hebrew calendar counts from what the Jewish people historically believed to be the time of creation—a date even earlier than the beginning of the Chinese calendar. The result? The year 2000 will be the Hebrew year 5760.

B.C. and A.D.

Many years ago, a Catholic monk had been given the task of figuring out when Jesus was born. When he gave his report to the pope, he added the words *anno Domini* ("in the year of our Lord") to a date that he had counted from the birth of Jesus—which the monk figured to be some five hundred years before. Since then, that Latin phrase has been abbreviated by writing A.D. to symbolize any date after the birth of Jesus. The abbreviation B.C. stands for "before Christ."

Today there are about forty different calendars in use around the world, usually to mark religious holy days and traditional festivals. No single one is more correct than the others because each serves its own purpose, but so many calendars could be confusing. You wouldn't want to get on a plane in New York in the year 2000 and arrive in China in the year 4698!

That's why almost everyone uses the same calendar and is celebrating the millennium. The millennium comes now because *this* calendar says it does.

I got your calendar right here, buddy!

But Why Did Calendars Start? Why Do People Need Them?

To understand calendars, we have to go back long before the Romans. . . .

People have always needed to know what would happen next in their world. Perhaps Stone Age people saw mammoths migrating when the moon was full and made a notch on a bone to note the event. Then they made a notch for each full moon after that until the mammoths migrated again. In time, they realized they could count full moons to predict when the mammoths would migrate.

Other "calendars" might have counted the moons from one winter to the next. These simple calendars helped people plan their lives.

All that counting and they didn't even have "M&M's"® to help them.

Later, when people started to farm, farmers and merchants carried their crops and goods to market. It did them no good if they arrived the day after market day. People needed to measure time with accurate calendars to track the days and months and years— and, eventually, millennia.

Gee, How Do You Make a Calendar?

The moon and the sun help.

Ancient people looked to the world around them for help setting up their calendars. For most, the moon provided answers. Its phases—the changing amount of light from the sun we can see on it—repeat themselves every twenty-nine or thirty days. These changes could easily be seen on clear nights and gave people the idea of a month.

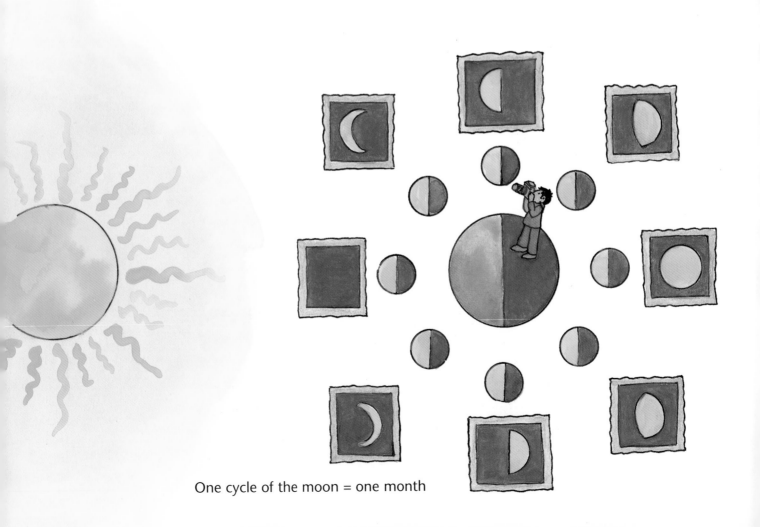

One cycle of the moon = one month

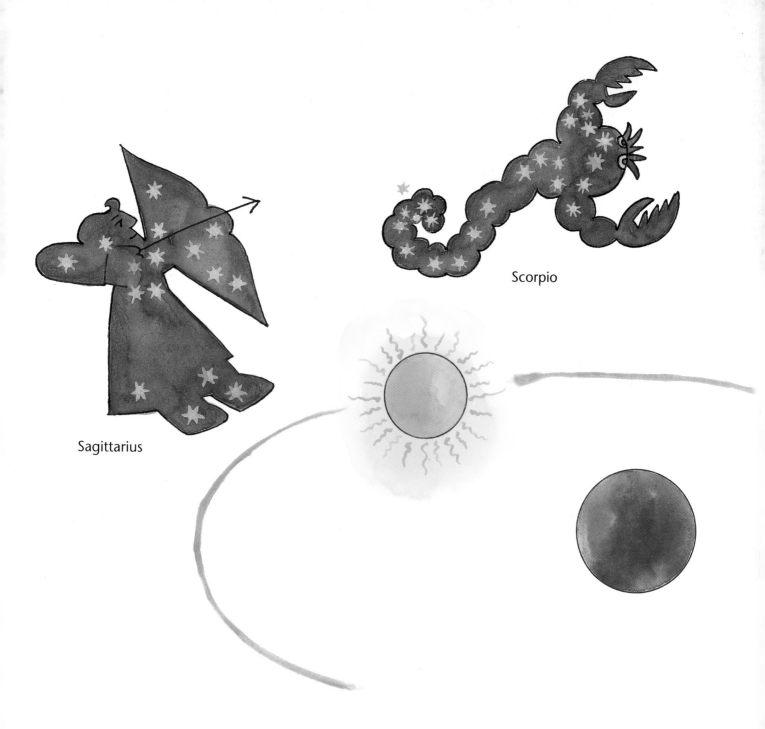

Scorpio

Sagittarius

In other places people ran their calendars by the stars and the sun. They connected the stars to make twelve pictures or constellations in the sky, which they named after animals and heroic figures. We know that the earth orbits the sun . . . but to many early people it looked as if the sun moved through these twelve constellations as it circled about the earth.

And now we call these constellations the zodiac.

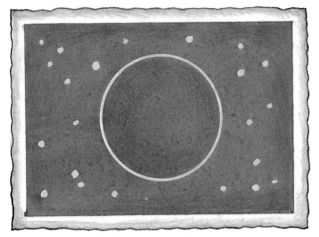

A new moon—a time when we cannot see sunlight on the moon.

The earliest calendars we know about followed the *lunar* cycle. Each new moon signaled the beginning of a new month.

The Babylonians (in what is now Iraq) soon discovered a small problem with a lunar calendar: It didn't stay lined up with the seasons. If it didn't, they might plant at the wrong time. So, by 432 B.C. they were using a new calendar that was sometimes twelve months long and sometimes thirteen months long. It was complicated, but it worked . . . until somebody couldn't remember if they should be using the twelve-month or thirteen-month calendar.

Accuracy wasn't the only problem with early calendars. All the calendars were different! Some places started each new year on the spring equinox—around March 21, when the number of hours of daylight equals the number of hours of darkness. But in Egypt the new year began in the middle of June. On top of that, some places began their day at sunset, while others began it at sunrise or midday. It must have been very confusing for travelers!

Sirius

Canis Major

At least they didn't have jet lag back in those days!

The Egyptians were the first to make a lunar calendar work better. Around 4000 B.C., they began to use a notched reed to measure the high-water mark of the Nile River—and discovered that the floods happened almost exactly one year apart. Then Egyptian priest-astronomers noticed that Sirius, the dog star, appeared in the predawn sky at the same time as the flood.

At the first sight of these two yearly events, priest-astronomers would declare a new year of three seasons: flooding, seed time, and harvest. And the count of months would begin again.

Most lunar calendars didn't follow the seasons at all. They alternated 6 months of 29 days each with 6 months of 30 days each. This added up to a year of 354 days.

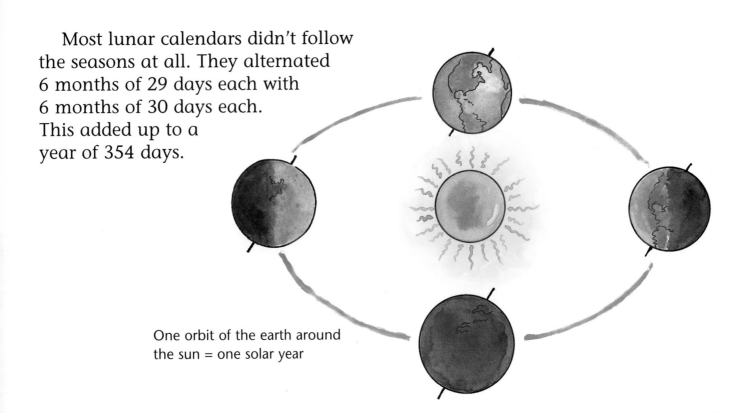

One orbit of the earth around the sun = one solar year

But the earth's tilt and its orbit around the sun make the seasons. A complete orbit—one year by the *solar* calendar—takes a little longer than 365 days. So, a lunar year of 354 days is 11 days short of a solar year. This meant that when people used a lunar calendar, months slowly drifted away from their original seasons. Eventually, "planting time" according to the calendar would be in the winter.

To fix the lunar calendars, people added extra days or stuck an extra month into the calendar every few years.

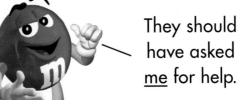

They should have asked <u>me</u> for help.

Hey, this calendar works pretty well!

The Chinese

The Chinese found a way to combine the lunar calendar with the solar year. Their *lunisolar* calendar began months on the new moon but added extra months every two or three years to stay in agreement with the seasons. This calendar is still in use.

Like many people, the Chinese saw pictures among the stars. They named their constellations after animals: rat, ox, tiger, hare, dragon, snake, horse, sheep, monkey, rooster, dog, and pig. Each animal influences the year it rules over. The year 2000 (year 4698 on the Chinese calendar) will be the year of the dragon, a time of excitement and complexity.

THE AZTECS

When the Aztecs conquered the Mayans, who lived in Central America, they adopted the Mayan calendar system for their own. The Aztec-Mayan system involved three separate calendars that were kept at the same time.

Can you imagine what their watches looked like?

The first calendar was based on a 365-day solar year. It was 18 months long, with 20 days to each month. To make 365 days, they added 5 extra days to the end of their year. Most Aztecs just wanted these 5 days to hurry and pass because they believed that they were unlucky.

The second calendar may have been connected to the movements of planets as well as the sun. It guided people in planting, harvesting, war making, and the offering of sacrifices.

To measure long periods of time, the Aztecs also had a Long Count calendar—a continuous numbering of all the days from a distant point in their past.

THE ROMANS

What about the calendar used in most of the world today? That smooth-running calendar comes from the Roman calendar, which in its early days did not run smoothly at all. Long ago, the Romans had an awkward ten-month year, less than three hundred days long. Around 700 B.C., they tried to make it work better by adding two months—Januarius and Februarius—and an extra day.

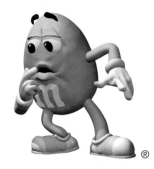

Wow, they just made it up as they went along!

How Many Days in a Week?

People invented what we call weeks as an amount of time longer than a day, but shorter than a month. In many places a week was the time between market days, but that amount of time varied. Early Rome had an eight-day week. Other places had six-day or even ten-day weeks.

How did we end up with a seven-day week? Before telescopes existed, when people observed the sky they saw only seven moving objects: the sun, moon, and five planets (Mercury, Venus, Mars, Jupiter, and Saturn). Each of these planet-gods ruled over a day. Once each god's day had passed, the cycle would repeat and a new week of seven days would begin.

Did this work? A twelve-month year was better than a ten-month year, but its 355 days still fell short of the solar year. What we call September didn't stay in the fall. So the Romans tried to fix that problem by adding an extra month to the end of February.

This could have worked, except it wasn't carefully managed. Rulers and priests added the extra month for their own gain—usually to stay in office longer.

Red-Letter Days
Special days in the eight-day Roman week were shown in red letters on the calendar. Some people think this is where we get our own term "Red-Letter Days." What do you think?

I think they named them after me!

After these "fixes," the Roman calendar soon got out of step again with the seasons. It took Julius Caesar to really fix it. War took him to Egypt, where he fell in love with the Egyptian queen, Cleopatra—and helped her take the Egyptian throne away from her brother.

Finally, some interesting trivia!

In Egypt, Caesar learned about the solar calendar the Egyptians used. Right away, he decided that the Roman Empire should use one, too.

People resist change, but Caesar was a powerful man. It's a good thing, too, because to make the new calendar work he had to do some bold things. First, he established 12 alternating months of 30 and 31 days. February had 29 days, but got an extra day every fourth year—a "leap year."

Once in a Blue Moon
Ever hear the expression "once in a blue moon"? Originally, it meant something that was very rare. That's because the moon only looks blue if there's a lot of dust or smoke in the air . . . say when a large volcano erupts. Recently, people started to use it to mean another rarity—the second full moon when a month has two.

Looks like rush hour!

Next, Caesar made the year 46 B.C. longer by more than two months. He had to, to bring the calendar back in step with the seasons. This turned the Roman world topsy-turvy: Shipping schedules were interrupted, contracts were disputed, and taxes were protested. Caesar's 445-day year, the longest in history, became "the Year of Confusion."

In the end, it worked. Rome finally had a calendar that kept pace with the seasons and was easy to manage. It was solar, almost identical to the Egyptian calendar. Later, the Roman Senate decided to honor Caesar by changing Quinctilis (the seventh month) to Julius. Imagine—if it weren't for Caesar, we wouldn't have July!

After Caesar's death his great-nephew Augustus came to power and wanted a month named after himself, too. He chose one that had been lucky for him. But it was only a 30-day month, and Caesar's month had 31 days. So Augustus took a day from February. That gave us August, but now poor February was left with only 28 days.

So they called this the Julian calendar—not bad, to get a calendar named after you!

QUINCTILIS
JULIUS

SEXTILIS
AUGUSTUS

The Julian calendar came close to working, but it was eleven minutes off the solar year. By 1582—long after the Roman Empire had ended—eleven minutes each year had added up to about ten days. Easter, a spring festival, might be celebrated in the wrong season!

To fix things, Pope Gregory XIII declared that October 5 would become October 15. Ten days were gone forever.

The pope also changed Caesar's leap-year rule. Every fourth year would still be a leap year, and years ending in 00 that could be evenly divided by 400 would be leap years, too. But if they could not be evenly divided by 400, they would have the usual 365 days. As a result, the year 2000 is a leap year, but 1900 was not.

The *Gregorian calendar* was adopted gradually all over the rest of the world. As time goes by, it will have to be corrected again; by 4909, it will be one whole day off.

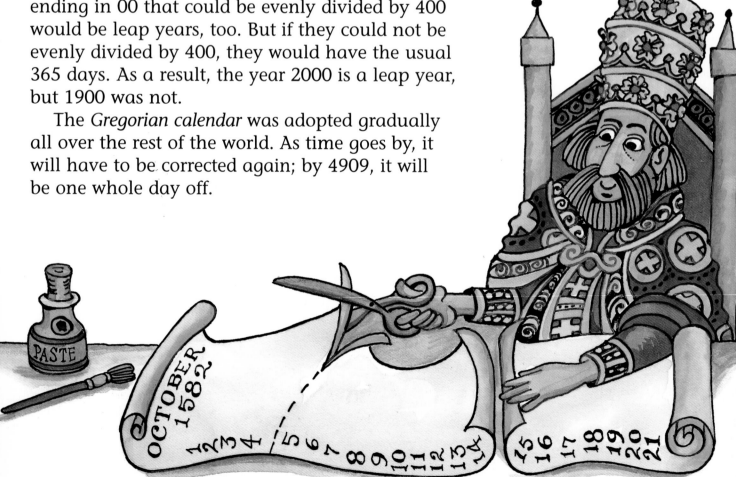

"Give Us Back Our Eleven Days"

The Pope's influence extended far and wide, but not into countries like Germany and England. These continued to use the Julian calendar. But 170 years later, England and its colonies finally started to use the Gregorian calendar—and they were among the last to do it.

By then, the date according to the English calendar was eleven days different from the rest of Europe. So, the English dropped them out of the calendar—Wednesday, September 2, 1752, was followed by Thursday, September 14. Some people thought the eleven days had been stolen from their lives! Employers refused to pay a full month's wages, landlords wanted a full month's rent, and mobs rioted in the streets. "Give us back our eleven days!" they cried.

Uh, did they really lose those days?

No, silly. They were only gone from the calendar.

So That's How It All Happened!

We have the Gregorian calendar,
and we've reached a millennium!

But what's the big deal?

Why *are* people so excited about the new millennium?
It may have to do with our number system, which goes back
to India over one thousand years ago. People there were the
first to use a number system of nine digits plus zero.

Now, ten and its multiples seem important to us.
A tenth, twentieth, or thirtieth birthday is a milestone
event. So is watching your car's odometer roll over to
50,000 or 100,000 miles. These things happen only once.
So it is with the millennium—10 centuries,
100 decades, 10 times 10 times 10 years!

1-2-3-4-5-6-7-8-9

Indian numbers
became what we now
call "Arabic numerals."
We still use them today,
because they are easier to work
with than Roman numerals.

5BC-4BC-3BC-2BC-1BC-1AD-2AD-3AD-4AD-5AD

But the millennium could easily have happened at a different time. If our years were lunar years of 354 days, our calendar could have reached the year 2063!

Or if our calendar had *started* at a different year, we'd get to the millennium at a different time!

Need more confusion? In the Gregorian calendar, we date time from A.D. 1. Going backward, we measure time from 1 B.C. There was no "zero" year. So, A.D. 1 through A.D. 1000 was the first millennium. By this countdown, the third millennium will begin on January 1, 2001, and not the year 2000.

Does it matter? Well, most people have settled on the time when the nines turn into zeroes—when 1999 turns into 2000.

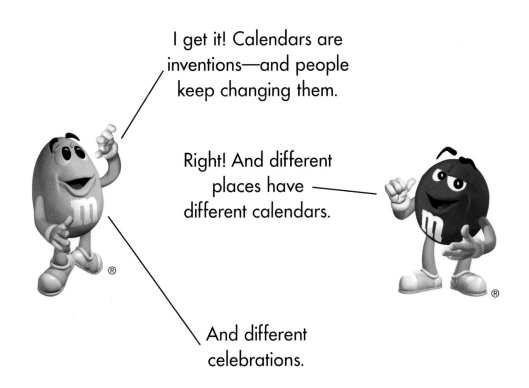

I get it! Calendars are inventions—and people keep changing them.

Right! And different places have different calendars.

And different celebrations.

OK, Time to Celebrate!
THAT'S What
the New Millennium Is!

As 1999 rolls over to 2000, some people are afraid computers will shut down because their programs cannot recognize the year 2000.

For most people, though, the millennium signals hope. They feel that age brings wisdom. They envision a better time coming: a world without misery and illness, a world where people live together in harmony.

But every age has had both doomsayers and optimists.

Only one thing is certain—on December 31, 1999, people will celebrate. . . .

In China, laser lights will illuminate the fourteen-hundred-year-old Great Wall.

In New York City, giant TV screens set up in Times Square will broadcast the arrival of the year 2000 in each of the world's twenty-four time zones.

Greenwich, England, will open the Millennium Dome, an entertainment complex, in the place that keeps official time for the world.

In Vatican City, the pope will preside over a churchwide jubilee and prayer vigil.

In Giza, Egypt, a music festival and light show will highlight the Great Pyramids.

In Bluff township, New Zealand, visitors will watch 1999's last sunset disappear over the Tasman Sea to the west and the first sunrise of 2000 a few hours later over the Pacific.

And in town squares everywhere . . . people will gather to welcome MM— the beginning of the next millennium.

MM—We have a big responsibility.

When the Millennium Is Over, What Comes Next?

Look back at the second millennium. Were there any changes? You bet. The second millennium changed in ways that people in the first millennium never expected. The invention of movable type and, much later, the computer, influenced the spread of information. The combustion engine and air flight had a profound impact on the way people work and travel. Rockets have allowed us to explore other worlds.

Some Second Millennium Inventions:

And colorful chocolate candies. Don't forget that!

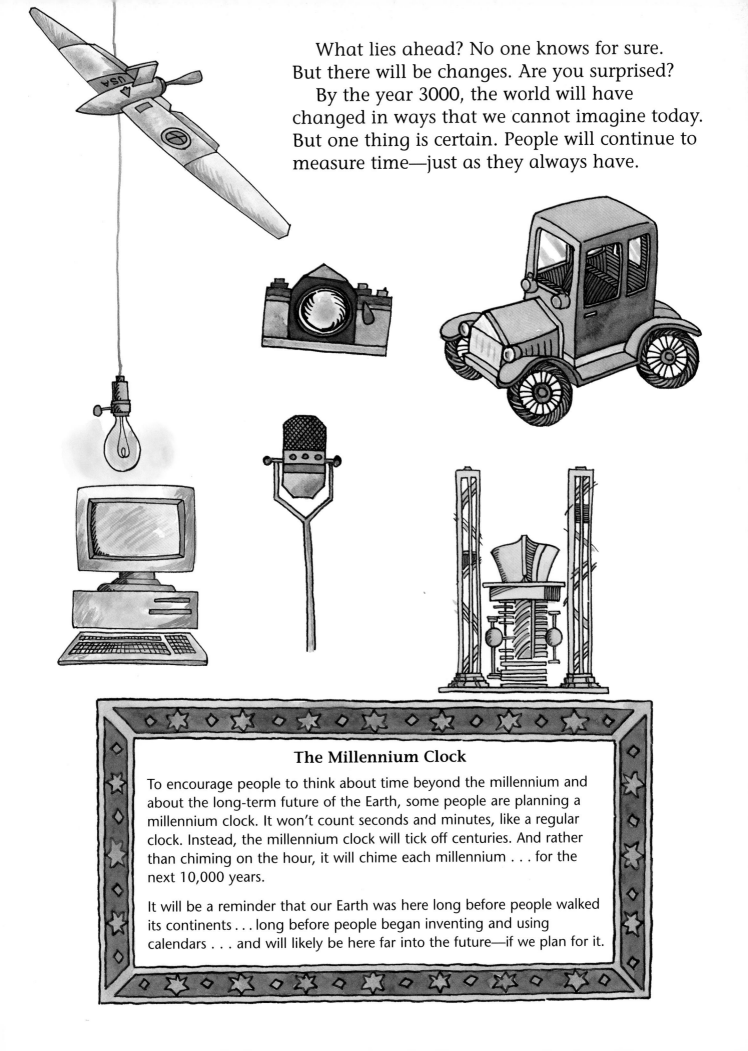

What lies ahead? No one knows for sure. But there will be changes. Are you surprised?

By the year 3000, the world will have changed in ways that we cannot imagine today. But one thing is certain. People will continue to measure time—just as they always have.

The Millennium Clock

To encourage people to think about time beyond the millennium and about the long-term future of the Earth, some people are planning a millennium clock. It won't count seconds and minutes, like a regular clock. Instead, the millennium clock will tick off centuries. And rather than chiming on the hour, it will chime each millennium . . . for the next 10,000 years.

It will be a reminder that our Earth was here long before people walked its continents . . . long before people began inventing and using calendars . . . and will likely be here far into the future—if we plan for it.

That's easy. You get geologic time.

This is what you call the Big Time!

EON

ERA

MILLIONS OF YEARS AGO

PERIOD

PHANEROZOIC EON

PALEOZOIC ERA

CAMBRIAN | ORDOVICIAN | 500 | SILURIAN | DEVONIAN | CARBONIFEROUS | 275 | PERMIAN | TRIASSIC

A year can seem like a long time when you are waiting for your next birthday. But is it? What about a decade? A decade is longer. So is a century. And a millennium—a thousand years—is the longest time of all . . .

. . . unless you consider that the earth has been around a lot longer than that. The earth is about 4.5 billion years old—that's about 4.5 million millennia! So scientists measure the age of the earth in geologic time. They invented eons (the longest divisions of geologic time) and eras (at least two to an eon) and periods (shorter than an era) and epochs (shorter than a period, but still thousands and thousands of years long).

So, given the big picture, a millennium isn't such a long time after all. It's just a few candles on Earth's enormous cake.

Is there a billennium?

An eon is a billion years—you could call that a billennium.

PHANEROZOIC EON

MESOZOIC ERA

CENOZOIC ERA

200

JURASSIC

CRETACEOUS

65

TERTIARY

QUATERNARY

PRESENT

LOWER CRETACEOUS

UPPER CRETACEOUS

← EPOCHS →

PALEOCENE

EOCENE

OLIGOCENE

MIOCENE

PLIOCENE

PLEISTOCENE

HOLOCENE

Bibliography and WWW Resources

Apfel, Necia H. *Calendars*. New York: Franklin Watts, 1985.

Dale, Rodney. *Timekeeping*. London: The British Library, 1992.

Evenson, A. E. *About the History of the Calendar*. Chicago: Children's Press, 1972.

Fakih, Kimberly Olson. *Off the Clock: A Lexicon of Time Words and Expressions*.
   Boston: Houghton Mifflin, 1995.

Mandell, Muriel. *Simple Experiments in Time with Everyday Materials*. New York:
   Sterling Publishing, 1997.

Wilson, Jerry. *"What Millennium Is It, Anyway?"*
   http://wilstar.net/millennium.htm
   Looks at when the third millennium begins and explains why there are
   differing opinions.

National Institute of Standards and Technology *"A Walk through Time"*
   http://physics.nist.gov/GenInt/Time/time.html

United States Naval Observatory *"Looking to the Year 2000 and Beyond."*
   http://psyche.usno.navy.mil/millennium
   Countdown to the millennium clock, 2000 vs. 2001, where the sun rises first
   on 01/01/2000, facts about the millennium page.

These two sites will show you how long until the new millennium,
whether it's January 1, 2000 or January 1, 2001:

Greenwich 2000. *"Greenwich 2000 Millennium Countdown Clock"*
   **http://millennium.greenwich2000.com/countdown/
   countdown2001.htm**
   How many hours, minutes, seconds left to the year 2001?

Heavelution Concert Productions Canada *"Calgary Canada's Count Down
   Clock to the New Millennium"*
   http://www.telusplanet.net/public/psamag/clock.htm
   How many hours, minutes, seconds left to the year 2000?

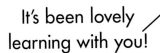

It's been lovely
learning with you!

It's the New Millennium!

A time of excitement, and some anxiety. . . . But just what is a millennium? Why is it happening? And why celebrate it?

You'll find the answers to these and many other questions here, with the "Official Candy of the New Millennium."™ Red® and Yellow® will be your guides. Learn about calendars and how they work—or don't work!—see how the sun and the moon have helped people keep track of time, take a look at red-letter days and blue moons, and find out how the particular calendar we use has arrived at a millennium now.

You Can't Spell Millennium Without An &

ISBN 0-88106-072-0